It's always a good idea to get to know your landlord

THE BEST BEERS AND CIDERS OF SOUTH WEST ENGLAND

Edward James

This edition is produced in collaboration with BBC Radio Bristol
and Somerset Sound, and is the inspiration for Radio Bristol's
series, "Time, Gentlemen Please" (produced by Peter Lawrence)
first broadcast in July and August 1994.

Text © 1994 by Broadcast Books, 4 Cotham Vale
Bristol BS6 6HR

Design and cartoons by Ed Crewe
Maps by Jules Lewis
Printed by Bath Press, Avon.

isbn: 1 874092 22 2

ACKNOWLEDGEMENTS

I would like to thank all the breweries and cider producers listed in the book, for their time and good will in giving me the information I needed. Also to be thanked are my colleague and co-founder of **Corks of Cotham**, Richard McCraith, for his patience while I was writing this book, the staff of the **Highbury Vaults** for letting us take the cover photograph in their front bar, and Lu Hersey for editing her way through the fruity, hoppy prose.

Picture Credits

Many of the breweries listed here kindly allowed me to include their labels and posters as illustrations in this book. In particular, I would also like to thank Vicky Coffingham and Laurence Sutherland of St. Austell's Brewery, for permission to reproduce the photographs on pages 8 and 97. The illustrations on page 97 is reproduced here by kind permission of H.P. Bulmer Ltd., page 59 courtesy of Hereford City Library, and pages 5,14,34,38,57,61,64 and 69 are from the extensive archives on the history of cider production at the Somerset Rural Life Museum, Glastonbury.

CONTENTS

INTRODUCTION

This is a guide to the amazing range and variety of bitters, porters, stouts and ciders made by independent producers throughout the South West of England. I have concentrated only on those products that, in my opinion, are of outstanding quality. I have also tried to make the guide as easy to use and jargon-free as possible, so that the occasional beer or cider drinker, or the tourist passing through this glorious region, will not feel intimidated by technical data.

The language used to describe alcoholic products is now a talking point across the country, made famous by television food and wine critics. People laugh and criticise, but it is important. The variety of alcoholic drinks is endless. There has to be a way of describing them. Some of the language in this book might seem over the top or too flowery, but if you try the beers and ciders I mention, and think about their descriptions, I think you'll begin to discern the elements of honey, nuts, hops, etc. coming through, although ultimately, perception of flavour is a personal experience. For this reason, there is no glossary enclosed to elaborate on these descriptions - which may come as a relief!

Brewing has a long history. The first beer-type product was brewed in Egypt over 4000 years ago. It was enjoyed by kings and slaves alike, and was even brewed for the gods, enclosed in the tombs of the pharaohs. In Europe the monasteries and convents of the Church developed secret beer and liquor production techniques throughout the Middle Ages, exposing the good fathers to the merciless satires of poets and songsters.

In Britain beer was developed from ale, a word derived from the Viking "øl" and Anglo-Saxon "ealu". Ale was a honey-fermented drink based on whatever grain crop was available. Throughout the Dark Ages this pallid brew was the main release for the English peasant, until the inspired introduction of "the wicked weed call'd hops" in the sixteenth century. This gave the drink a new, "bitter" flavour – hence the word "beer". From then on, brewing in Britain never looked back, until a sad slump in the quality and variety of beers which coincided with the rise of mass beer production after the Second World War. To a large extent, CAMRA (the Campaign for Real Ale) has fostered not only a beer revival but a new public awareness of, and demand for, quality beers. With this revival comes a new sense of pride and means of survival for the small, independent breweries.

Every brewer mentioned in the Guide has two things in common – a love of his craft and a desire to give value to the customer. Rarely have I encountered anyone "in it for the money", which is just as well, because the financial burden on the small brewer is considerable. They are continually struggling against takeover bids from the big breweries, and ever-rising costs on top of the production problems they face as traditional brewers. In addition, the tax on alcohol is levied at the same rate on every brewer, from the largest conglomerate to the smallest independent. There are no concessions made on level of turnover or size of output, unlike those made available to our continental competitors. It is not only the small breweries that suffer – the UK consumer pays the second highest drink duty in the whole of the EC, eight times that of France! I do not know how long this situation can continue, especially as these price anomalies have given rise to the recent extraordinary quantities of cheap beers imported from Belgium and France, van-loads at a time by day trippers.

The quality of a pint of cider is more difficult to define. We all know what we don't admire – the uniform, fizzy, gutless product of the big cider plants which nevertheless has become such a marketing success with young drinkers. Just as in the 1960's an ailing manufacturer of perry reinvented his drink as 'Babycham'; a new image has been created for commercially produced cider – clean, crisp, filtered, in preposterous little bottles, with prices to match. But what is true of good beer is equally true of good cider, perry, or wine. A natural product cannot be mass-produced. A good cider will always taste of pure apples, no matter how strong – and all the ciders listed have a strength of between 6 - 8%. This is one reason why cider can seem such an innocent drink, with such deadly results!

Cider production has changed over the last seventy years. Once almost every farm in the South West had a few cider apple trees to make a rough cider which would slake the thirst of the farm labourers, and formed part of their wages. The quantities drunk were astonishing – several gallons per man per day was quite normal, and a cider-drinker's career began early. Toddlers were often pacified with a mug full! Gradually production fell away as farm workers found more lucrative employment in the towns after the Second World War. Orchards were uprooted to clear fields for cash crops – or, more recently, for holiday chalets and caravans.

Almost too late, the EC has recently introduced legislation to encourage the planting of cider and perry orchards again, and nowhere are conditions more favourable for these crops than in the South West. Some would argue stubbornly that only Somerset produces the optimum weather and soil conditions to grow cider apples! But it takes time to mature a cider orchard. The older the tree, the better the fruit. The better the fruit, the more apple flavoured and potent the cider. That is why the cider producers listed in this Guide are not newcomers to cider production, but have carried on the tradition of their grandfathers and great-grandfathers, against the general agricultural trend of the century. Their ciders are all good, and hence have not been graded as have the beers in this guide. However they are not marketing whizz kids. Many of these ciders are sold only on the farm, to appreciative locals. Many are struggling against the commercial products without vast advertising budgets to back them. Despite CAMRA's recent interest in cider as well as beer, the cider makers are for the most part an uncoordinated force, often suspicious of outside interference. Their future is uncertain. Yet who, having tasted a traditionally made cider, could ever drink something out of a designer bottle again?

Well-brewed traditional ale and cider are perhaps the most satisfying drinks there are. We owe a great debt of gratitude to these independent producers. Thank goodness for all those marvellous products with silly names like 'Cockle Roaster', 'Dirty Dick', 'Headbanger', 'Blewitts Headoff' or 'Whistle Belly Vengeance'... I don't look forward to the day when I might have to go to the bar, swallow my pride and shout, "Landlord, a pint of your dishwater, light, fizzy lager please." It is up to us not to let this happen. We should to travel the countryside, seek out the products of independent breweries and cider makers, buy them, and enjoy them for what they are. It would be our great loss if they were no longer available.

Recommended Visits

Most of the breweries and cider producers listed welcome visitors; Also especially recommended are visits to the Hereford Cider Museum, Hereford, and the Somerset Museum of Rural Life, Glastonbury.

Good beer is best savoured without accompaniment

CORNWALL

(Numbers relate to the map overleaf)

Mead Producers

③ Cornish Mead Company

Beer Breweries

④ Blue Anchor

① Redruth

② St. Austell

⑤ Tintagel

Cider Producers

Apple Blossom ②

Cornish Scrumpy Co. ①

Hay Farm ⑤

Pen Pol ③

Really Foul Cider Co. ④

Cornwall

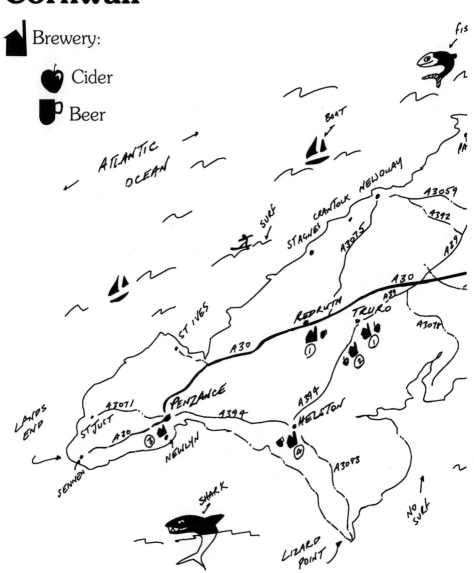

Brewery:

Cider

Beer

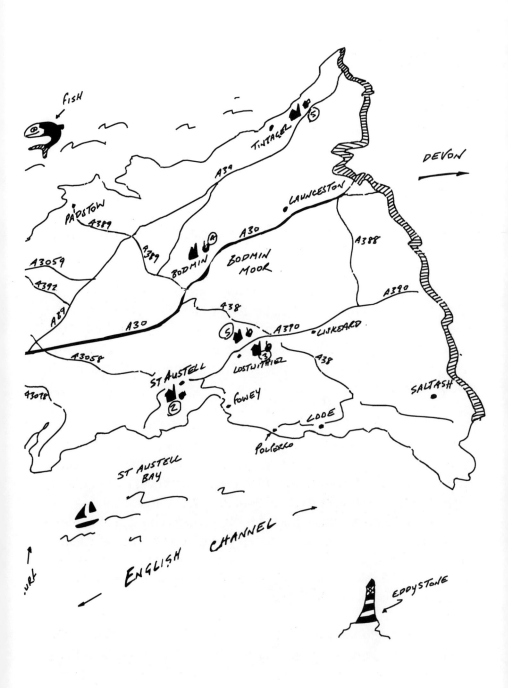

FISH

DEVON

TINTAGEL ⑤

LAUNCESTON

A39

PADSTOW

A389

A30

A388

A3059

A389

BODMIN ④

BODMIN MOOR

A392

A390

A89

A38

A30

⑤ ⑥

A390

LISKEARD

A3058

LOSTWITHIEL ③

A38

SALTASH

ST AUSTELL

A3078

②

FOWEY

LOOE

POLPERRO

ST AUSTELL BAY

ENGLISH CHANNEL

SURF

EDDYSTONE

The Cornish Mead Company
The Meadery
Newlyn
Penzance
Cornwall

Tel.: 0736 63942

Mead is a truly British drink with a history stretching back through medieval England to pagan times. Now in the twentieth century, the UK's leading mead producer is based in the far west of England, in Cornwall.

Cornish liqueur mead has a light grape-wine base and is flavoured with honey and fortified with brandy. It can be served alone but mixes well with gin, vodka or rum and makes a delicious long drink with lemon juice, bitter lemon or tonic water – although the latter three are not strongly recommended as they ruin the rather exotic flavour of true mead.

The two basic styles are Cornish Mead Wine and Cornish Liqueur Mead, the Liqueur Mead being significantly sweeter and commonly known as the honeymoon drink. Both products have a lusciously rich flavour and an after-taste which goes on forever. I particularly prefer the Cornish Mead Wine which has an interesting, nutty fragrance and a very long finish on the palate. The Cornish Mead Company also produces a range of fruit-flavoured meads: blackberry, elderberry, strawberry, peach, apricot and cherry. These are based on the lighter style of mead, not the liqueur type, but with amazing fruit flavours. Well worth a try!

The recommended place to try the whole range of meads is The Good Knight Meaderies in the town and nearby. These are Elizabethan-style eating houses, and well worth a try if you are feeling in the mood to tear a roast chicken apart with your bare hands – not as unlikely as you might think after a long drive into this remotest toe of England. The Bodmin Meadery in Bodmin is also well worth a visit. It has been converted from the old courthouse in Bodmin and you can sit in the original judge's chair to try the products, but beware, as they are deceptively strong. Driving is not recommended after a full tasting!

Rating: 🍷 🍷 🍷 🍷 🍷

(due to uniqueness of product)

An antique horn drinking beaker with a silver rim (3 inches high),
which would have been used to drink mead or cider.

BEERS

The Blue Anchor Brewery and Pub
50 Coinagehall Street
Helston
Cornwall
TR13 8EL

Tel.: 0326 562821

Beers produced:	Original Gravity
Medium Bitter	1050^0
Best Bitter	1053^0
Special Bitter	1066^0
Extra Special	1076^0

Beer has been brewed in Helston since the 14th century, the original brewing done by monks. The Blue Anchor stands on the monastery site and has been in the hands of one family for 150 years. Today it is run by Simon Stone.

During the summer they brew up to 30 barrels a week, which makes it necessary to arrive early if you want to have a seat in this tiny ancient pub . It gets very busy but is well worth a visit. An overnight stay in Helston is recommended due to the strength of the beers.

The **Medium Bitter** (so called!) at 1050 gravity is a wonderful beer. A full flavour, rich with nuts and tobacco – highly recommended.

The **Best Bitter** I found not as good, though having said that, a very pleasant tipple, slightly lighter in style and lacks a bit of backbone, but not a bad pint for the summer.

The **Special Bitter** I consider to be their star beer. Voluptuous rich flavour, slightly honeyed, with a wonderful full malty flavour – watch out, it's strong!

Even stronger is the **Extra Special**. Very similar style, a lot more alcohol – definitely a knockout brew, but after a cold swim in the sea there's nothing better to warm you up and get the circulation going.

Rating:

Redruth Brewery
Foundary Row
Redruth
Cornwall
TR10 8LA

Tel.: 0209 212244

Beers produced: **Original Gravity**
    Cornish Original   **1037⁰**

A former Cornish Steam Brewery, originally owned by Devonish and bought out by the management when Devonish stopped producing. An independent brewery but producing for Whitbread, mainly packaged beer for retail.

A dry malty beer with a slight fruit flavour, very much on the lighter side of ale, but not a bad pint. I think it might be interesting if they could produce something a little bit stronger.

Rating:

The Landlord of the Queen's Head, St. Austell

St. Austell Brewery Company Ltd.
63 Trevarthian Road
St. Austell
Cornwall
PL25 4BY

Tel.: 0726 74444

Beers produced:	Original Gravity
Bosuns Bitter	1034^0
XXXX Mild	1037^0
Tinners Ale	1041^0
Hicks Special	1053^0

Founded in 1851 by Walter Hick, St. Austell is one of the larger independent brewers still managing to maintain good cask-conditioned ale. Many say the distinctive flavour comes from the original secret spring coming from china clay enriched earth. A personal favourite of mine, these beers are well worth trying for the true taste of Cornwall. Although bottled beers are not the province of this guide, I must make one detour and mention **Cripple Dick**, extremely rich and strong – almost a barley wine. One Cripple Dick drinker recognises another by the secret sign of the wilted holly leaf, available as a discreetly embroidered motif on sweat shirts on sale at the brewery. The brewery shows a video of its history and brewing traditions, and is well worth a visit.

Bosuns Bitter is a popular lunchtime pint, this well-balanced traditional bitter is light in flavour and is excellent value for money.

XXXX Mild has a sweet malt flavour in the mouth and is one of the few remaining draught milds in the country. A proud winner of one of CAMRA's 1990 Best Beer awards.

Tinners Ale is the most popular of the traditional draught ales. Tinners is a cask-conditioned bitter of character, dry hopped and of medium strength.

Hicks Special has a biscuity, chalk flavour in the mouth with full fruit and hops finish. Known as Hicks Sudden Death to the locals, for obvious reasons. It's named after its founder.

The London Inn in Padstow is in the back streets of the village. It's highly recommended to try the range. You get the true atmosphere of Cornwall, although only small, a great pub with great service.

Rating:

The Tintagel Brewery
Min Pin Inn
Tregatta
Tintagel
Cornwall
PL3 40D

Tel.: 0840 770241

Beers produced:	Original Gravity
Legend Bitter	1035^0
Brown Willy Bitter	1055^0

Tintagel Brewery is an all female brewery. Marie Hall is a brewer, or brewster, and famed dog-breeder, having won awards at Crufts. The Brewery and pub are very small and you are unlikely to find the ales in other venues, so you could say she has a captive audience. The beers are good in this male-dominated industry.

Legend Bitter is a lovely bitter for the strength, very well made, very good flavour, lovely full malty and hoppy taste – highly recommended.

Brown Willy Bitter is not so good unfortunately, over strength for the quality and fruit content of the beer, but worth a try.

Note: Sadly, since researching the book, Marie Hall was forced to close the brewery. However I think honourable mention should be made of her venture, because of the bravery of the enterprise and quality of her products. With luck both may be revived.

Rating:

St. Austell Brewery's Cripple Dick

CIDERS

Apple Blossom Cider
The Cornish Cider Company
Trevean Farm
Coombe Lea
Near Truro
Cornwall

Tel.: 0872 77177

Ciders produced:
  Medium sweet and Medium Scrumpy

Apple Blossom cider is not available at the premises to be sold to the public, but a number of off-licenses in the vicinity stock the product, including the local chemist! The cider is fully traditional, and is mainly a blend of the famous Kingston Black Cider and Bramley apples. The result is a very well balanced drink.

Cornish Scrumpy Company Ltd.
Callestock Cider Farm
Penhallow
Truro
Cornwall

Tel.: 0872 573356

Ciders produced:
  Dry, Medium Dry and Medium Sweet

Cornish Scrumpy is sold all over Cornwall, but it is well worth a visit to the cider farm itself to see their shop and production and, obviously, to try their great products. There's much to see at the farm, from displays on the history of cider making, to making a trip round the present plant. The size of the fermentation tanks, each holding 23000 litres, will amaze you and the blend of old methods and new is quite impressive.

The use of champagne yeast ensures consistency in the products and the products are worthy of a high rating. This is true natural Cornish scrumpy at its very best. The posters proclaiming "Cornish Scrumpy, legless but smiling" are not joking!

Cornish Scrumpy's truthful advertising slogan

Hay Farm Cider
St. Vepp
Near Lost Withiel
Cornwall

Tel.: 0208 872250

Ciders produced:
   Real Cider

The product can be tried and purchased on the premises. It contains a blend of no less than fifteen different apple varieties. This is a crisp, well-made cider, with a great body, but not too strong. A great summer drink.

The first process in the production of cider is the apple milling. The photograph on the left shows how it was conducted at the turn of the century.
The wooden shovel in the foreground was used since metal would dissolve in the cider and thus taint it.

Pen Pol Cider
Middle Pen Pol Farm
St. Veep
Near Lost Withiel
Cornwall

Tel.: 0208 872017

Ciders produced:
　　Medium Cider

Although only a small producer, the cider is well worth trying. A wonderful full appley taste, expertly made on this very small farm. Cider can be bought from the farm. Remember to take your own container – marketing is not a strong point here!

Really Foul Cornish Cider Company
Bodmin
Cornwall

Tel.: 0208 82431

Don't be fooled by the name, the cider's great! Amazing flavours again, but only using the famous Kingston Black apple. Cider cannot be purchased on the premises. A worthy place to try the product is the Trengilly Wartha Inn, which can be found at the head of the Helford River. A great cider.

DEVON

(Numbers relate to the map overleaf)

Beer Breweries

⑥ The Beer Engine
② Black Awton Brewery
⑩ Blewitt's Brew Pub
⑤ Branscombe Vale Brewery
⑦ Exe Valley Brewery
⑨ Fergusons Plymouth
    Brewery
④ The Mill Brewery
⑧ Otter Brewery Ltd.
① Summerskills Brewery
③ The Tallyho Country
    Inn and Brewery

Cider Producers
Abbey Gate ⑫
Brimblecombes ⑬
Brommels ⑨
Churchwards ⑩
Clarks Farmhouse ⑪
Dead Dick's ⑦
Farmer John's ⑧
Gray's Farm ④
Hancocks ⑤
Home House ⑮
Inches ⑯
Luscoombe ⑥
Palmershayes ①
Reed's ③
Redderways Farm ②
Yearlstone ⑭

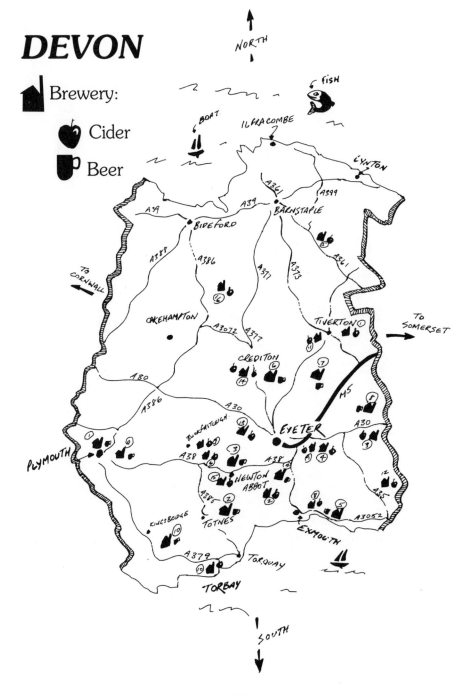

DEVON

Brewery:

Cider

Beer

BEERS

The Beer Engine
Newton St. Cyres
Exeter
Devon

Tel.: 0392 851282

Beers Produced:	Original Gravity
Rail Ale	1037^0
Piston Bitter	1044^0
Sleeper Heavy	1059^0
Whistlemass	1068^0

Peter Hawksley runs and owns this brew/pub next door to the railway line in the countryside near Exeter. He started approximately eleven years ago, and last year he produced his millionth pint of beer. The pub has a great reputation for excellent food as well as fine beers, which are so renowned that in 1993 he was invited to show them in France, where they went down very well.

Rail Ale is a light, refreshing ale with a full malt and hoppy flavour.

Piston Bitter has a full flavour. The malt and hops last in the mouth forever. The finish is big and chocolatey, with a slight bitterness. Amber-coloured.

Sleeper Heavy enjoys full chocolate and coffee aromas. This is a dark, strong ale, also available to the free trade.

Whistlemass is a very strong, rich tasting, hoppy ale. Not always available, but when it is, well worth a try.

19

Rating:

Black Awton Brewery
Washbourne
Totnes
Devon

Tel.: 0804 23339

Beers Produced:	Original Gravity
Black Awton Bitter	1037^0
Devon Gold	1040^0
Forty Four Special	1044^0
Headstrong	1051^0

This independent brewery produces an interesting range of beers. Unfortunately it is not open for visiting, but is sold in the majority of pubs in the area.

Black Awton Bitter is a very fresh, floral beer with a woody end. A copper-coloured bitter.

Devon Gold. Again, a beer of light aroma with bigger hoppy nose, slightly sweet palate with resin on the finishing aroma. A pale beer, for lager drinkers.

Forty Four Special is a beer with more depth. It has a full hop and malt aroma, with a long after taste. It is very well balanced, and slightly fruity – a mellow product.

Headstrong. A strong mild-style beer, dark in presentation with a

large amount of sweetness and jam. Not enough acidity and malty flavour – a slightly unbalanced product.

Rating:

Blewitt's Brew Pub
Ship and Plough
Kingsbridge
South Devon

Tel.: 0548 852485

Beers Produced:	Original Gravity
Blewitt's Best Bitter	1040^0
Blewitt's Headoff	1050^0
Kings Bitter	1038^0

Steve Blewitt, the owner and brewer has experience indeed. He originally started brewing with his father's help at the tender age of ten in his mother's kitchen, where the steaming concoctions stripped the wallpaper. Popping and rumbling jars were stacked around his bedroom as well... He has since diversified and expanded, and with a ninety gallon copper made to his own design produces some lovely beers.

Blewitt's Best Bitter has a lovely, light golden amber colour and texture and taste – finishes with a very hoppy aroma.

Blewitt's Head Off is, as the name suggests, noticeably stronger, with a similar look to the Blewitt's Best Bitter but a touch more body, and yeast coming through on the finish.

Due to supply I was unable to taste the Kings, but am much looking forward to it, judging by the rest of his products.

Rating:

Branscombe Vale Brewery
Great Seaside Farm
Branscombe
Devon

Tel.: 0297 80511

Beers Produced:	Original Gravity
Brannoc	1040^0
Old Stoker	1055^0

Set idyllically on the coast, the brewery is housed in two barns. It is run by Graham Luxton and Paul Diamond, and Graham's wife runs the local pub, the Branscombe Village Inn.

Brannoc is a full, rich, malty beer with a very long finish, and slightly acidic on the end. It is pale, but well balanced.

Old Stocker is a dark, rich beer with a slight chocolatey under-taste. Very malty on the bouquet and full-flavoured, with hints of yeast.

Rating:

Exe Valley Brewery
Silverton
Near Exeter
Devon

Tel.: 0392 860408

Beers produced:	Original Gravity
Exe Valley Bitter	1038^0
Dobb's Best Bitter	1041^0
Devon Glory	1047^0
Exeter Old Bitter	1047^0

The brewery has been run by Richard Baron and Gary Sheppard since 1984. The beers are all made with malt, hops and natural spring water from a local spring, with no additives. The Exeter Old Bitter won the Strong Bitter class at the 1993 Great British Beer festival. The products can all be tried at the Silverton Inn, a pleasant and friendly pub.

Exe Valley Bitter is a powerful, hoppy beer with a long nutty finish, pale and slightly astringent on the finish.

Dobb's Best Bitter is a smooth, full-bodied beer with a lovely malty character. Slightly honeyed.

Devon Glory is a well made, full-flavoured beer with a lovely rich yeasty and malty aroma. A warming, full pint.

Exeter Old Bitter was not available for sampling at the time.

Rating:

Fergusons Plymouth Brewery
Valley Road
Plymouth
Devon

Tel.: 0752 330171

Beers Produced:	Original Gravity
Dartmoor Best Bitter	1038^0
Dartmoor Strong	1044^0
Cockle Roaster	1060^0

Although Plympton Brewery is still independent in style, it is unfortunately now a subsidiary of the ever-expanding Carlsberg Tetley. Despite this, the beers are still very good and produced in

Two of the beer mats commonly found in pubs serving Fergusons Plymouth beer

traditional manner. It is well worth a visit to the brewery, but arrange an appointment first.

Dartmouth Best Bitter has a light hoppy flavour with a slight aroma of nuts, a very dry finish with a slight toffeed end. A light amber beer.

Dartmouth Strong is very well balanced in flavour. A full, rich aroma and a slight citrus finish makes it well worth trying.

Cockle Roaster is a full winter warmer with a big yeasty nose. There is a huge malt and fruit flavour in your mouth, dying off to a fruity finish. Pale, but very powerful beer.

Rating:

The Mill Brewery
Unit 18c
Hanbury Buildings
Bradley Lane
Newton Abbot
Devon

Tel.: 0626 63322

Beers Produced:	Original Gravity
Janners Ale	1038^0
Janners Old Original	1045^0
Janners Christmas Ale	1050^0

Dave Hedge and his friend, Paul Bigrig, started the brewery in 1982 brewing only part-time, ten barrels a week, while keeping down full time careers. This is a tiny brewery tucked away behind and almost beneath a masonry yard. In March 1994 they sold the business to Mike and Liz Cox, who plan to brew occasional beers as well as the Janners, while keeping up the same excellent standards. The beers are named after a popular name for Devonians – "Janners".

Janners Ale is a true bitter. It has a very dry, rich hop aroma and a very malt, chocolatey and nutty flavour. Deep bitter finish.

Janners Old Original is a fuller, richer beer with a very full malt flavour. Deeply satisfying on the end and fruits that last forever in the mouth.

During the Christmas season the Old Original is brewed to a greater strength and called **Janners Christmas Ale.**

Rating:

Otter Brewery Ltd.
Maythayes
Luppitt
Honiton
Devon

Tel.: 0404 891285

Beers Produced:	Original Gravity
Otter Bitter	1036^0
Otter Ale	1044^0
Otter Head	1055^0

David McCraig originally trained as a brewer with Whitbreads. He started the Otter Brewery in 1990. He was lucky to find a disused barn next door, where with his own labours he created the Otter Brewery. Interestingly, he cultivates his own yeast. The beers are full-flavoured and very well made, and have a near national distribution, although only producing approximately twenty-five barrels a week. Interesting techniques make the brewery well worth a visit, but please phone for an appointment.

Otter Bitter is a well balanced beer showing great finesse. Full hoppy flavour on the nose.

Otter Ale is a richer, fruitier beer with a deep satisfying flavour and a dark, rich colour.

Otter Head has a rich, malty and hoppy aroma with a distinctive yeasty finish. A ripe, dark beer in the mouth, and strong with complex flavours.

Rating:

A poster for one of Summerskills appetisingly named beers

Summerskills Brewery
Unit 15
Promphlett Farm Industrial Estate
Broxton Drive
Billacombe
Plymouth
Devon
PL97BG

Tel.: 0752 481283

Beers Produced:	Original Gravity
Summerskills Best Bitter	1042⁰
Whistle Belly Vengeance	1046⁰
Ninja Beer	1049⁰
Indiana's Bones	1055⁰

Purchased by Carl Beeson and Rich Wilson in October 1990, within three years the distribution had expanded amazingly under the laid-back idiosyncratic style of this pair. They even export to the Channel Islands now.

Summerskills Best Bitter was one of the independently produced beers to have been drunk in the House of Commons bar, as part of the SIBA (Small Independent Breweries Association) campaign to bring these excellent national products to the attention of the government, and hopefully encourage a reduction in taxation for small breweries. So far SIBA has not had much success on this issue, although every month a different brewery is graciously permitted to take its turn to refresh the Honourable Members... The pale bitter, with a fine crystal malt and hops character, a full malt flavour in the mouth and aromas of rich malt, nuts and hops with a hint of honey.

Whistle Belly Vengeance is a dark ruby beer full of dark malt character, aromas of rich dark malt and hops, the mouth is dominated with hops, dark malt and liquorice.

Ninja Beer is a dark golden beer, well balanced with malt and hops, a taste of soft malt hops and toffee, with a light malt and hops aroma.

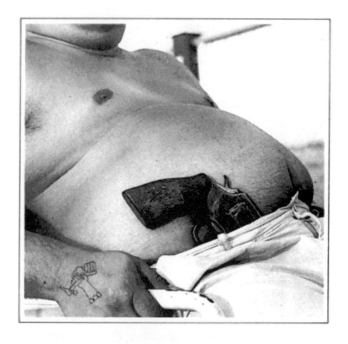

SUMMERSKILLS
PLYMOUTH
WHISTLE BELLY VENGEANCE

Indiana Bones is the newest edition, launched in November 1993, very much a winter ale. A rich, dark, winter warmer, soft chocolate in the mouth with characteristic golding aromas.

Rating:

The Tallyho Country Inn and Brewery
14 Market Street
Hatherleigh
Devon

Tel.: 0837 810306

Beers Produced:	Original Gravity
Potboiler Brew	1036⁰
Nutters	1048⁰
Tarka Triple	1048⁰
Thurgia	1056⁰

This is a wonderful pub/brewery with a very traditional feel, great food and very good beer. The owners are Italian, so there is also a fine range of Italian wines on the premises. The pub has a very traditional English feel, with oak panelling and very comfortable seats. Well worth a stay over.

Potboiler Brew has a wonderful, rich, malty aroma with hints of chocolate and nuts in the palate. A very fine hoppy character. A light-coloured beer with good malty nose.

Nutters is a beer with a huge malty aroma. It is a dark grain beer, very chocolatey, with a slight bitter coffee taste.

31

Tarka Triple is a wonderful cask and bottle condition brew. Very hoppy and dry in the mouth, with a long finish, and a subtle hint of chocolate.

Thurgia is literally translated from the Greek "natural magic". A very satisfying bottle-conditioned beer which has a limited allocation per annum. It has a slight bitter finish with a full hops and sultana fruit flavour. Dark brown in appearance.

Rating:

CIDERS

Abbey Gate Cider
Abbey Gate Farm
Musbury Road
Axminster
Devon

Tel.: 0297 33541

Ciders Produced:
    Medium and Dry

Visitors are welcome, although it is advisable to telephone first if you are coming a long way. Only 1000 gallons of cider are produced each year, so it's well worth visiting early in the season to make sure of your supplies! Ciders are produced using only local apples from neighbouring orchards. They are well made, with a full, crisp, appley flavour. The Medium in particular has quite a lot of biting acidity.

Brimblecombes Devon Farmhouse Cider
Farrants Farm
Dunsford
Devon

Tel.: 0392 81456

Ciders produced:
    Dry, Medium and Sweet cider

This is cider made in the traditional manner – the first cider was pressed on the farm almost 400 years ago. Purely old techniques are used producing full flavoured, cloudy, orange-coloured cider. The ciders are very rich in flavour, particularly the sweet.

Brommels Devon Farm Cider
Lower Uppercot
Teburn St. Mary
Near Exeter
Devon

Tel.: 0647 6294

A 30,000 gallons a year production is quite a feat considering that all apples come from within ten miles of the farm. The cider is strong and well made with an accentuated fruit flavour – recommended.

The 'Cooper's shop' of Whiteways of Whimple, around 1910

Churchwards Cider
Yalpeton Farm
Paignton
Devon

Tel.: 0803 558157

Ciders Produced:
Sweet, Medium and Dry.

Run by three sisters who took over the farm from their parents, the farm is well worth visiting for its award-winning ciders made from local apples, and to see the enormous, happy-looking prize pigs grazing under the cider apple trees! Also on sale is a tasty range of local produce. The farm can be very busy, but it's an absolute must for the cider fan. Very flavoursome appley ciders – among the best in the guide.

Clarks Farmhouse Cider
Shortridge Hill
Seven Crosse
Tiverton
Devon

Tel.: 0884 252632

Ciders Produced:
Medium and Dry

The cider here is made by Lawrence Clark, who treats it very much as a hobby. The ciders are well made and have distinctive flavours. A slight woodyness comes through on all styles. Again, all apples come from local farms.

Dead Dick Scrumpy
Dead Dick's Cider Company
The Smuggler's Layer
32 Fore Street
Buckfastleigh
Devon

Tel.: 0364 43095

Ciders produced:
Dead Dick Scrumpy, Bosun's Willys, Medium Sweet and Dry

The cider farm itself is not open to the public, but purchases can be made through local off-licences on the coast. The cider is produced from local apples in the traditional manner, and despite the pitch to tourists it is very well made, and very flavoursome. An excellent cider, to be taken seriously.

Farmer John's Devonshire Farmhouse Cider
Parsons Farm
Newton Poppleford
Near Sidmouth
Devon

Tel.: 0395 68152

Ciders produced:
Original Vintage Cider and Old Rascal Scrumpy

An age-old family tradition produces this marvellous cider. The Vintage Cider is a fairly sophisticated cider, with an interesting citrus finish. The Scrumpy Cider is slightly rough around the edges and not to be taken lightly. A good visit.

Gray's Farm Cider
Malston
Tedburn St Mary
Near Exeter
Devon

Tel.: 0647 61236

Ciders Produced:
Sweet, Medium and Dry

Cider has been made here by the Gray family for over 300 years, and is stored in the old cellar underneath the building. It's very well made, very potent, and consistent in flavour. The Grays produce over 20,000 gallons per annum.

Hancocks Devon Cider
Trentworthy Mill
South Molton
Devon

Tel.: 0769 52678

Ciders Produced:
Medium Sweet Cider, Medium Dry Cider, Medium Sweet Scrumpy and Dry Scrumpy

Hydraulic presses have been installed for over 50 years, and the ciders themselves have won over forty awards. A worthy visit, as everything can be tried on site.

Travelling cider making equipment from the Dulverton area

Home House Cider
Home House
Combeinteignhead
Near Newton Abbot
Devon

Tel.: 0626 872591

Ciders Produced:
Medium and Dry Cider

Cider production is more of a hobby here than a serious income, although Mr. and Mrs. Malpin produce 250 gallons a day in the season. The cider is well made and full flavoured, and surprisingly strong.

Inches Cider
Inches Cider Company
Western Barn
Hatherleigh Road
Winkley
Devon

Tel.: 0837 83363

Ciders Produced:
Sweet, Medium, Dry, Scrumpy and Pipkin Vintage
Scrumpy

Originally started in 1916 by Sam Inch, something in the region of a million gallons are produced each year. A management buy-out took on the business in 1989 and although independent, Inches is now nationally available. The products are good, consistent and certainly Devon folk are devotees.

Luscombe Cider
Luscombe Farm
Buckfastleigh
Devon

Tel.: 0364 42373

Cider Produced:
   Dry cider

The cider is well made, has a golden flavour and a woody nose. Visits are not accommodated well, but the cider is available in local off-licences.

Palmershayes Cider
Calverleigh
Near Tiverton
Devon

Tel.: 0884 254579

Ciders Produced:
   Sweet, Medium and Dry

Visits are welcomed, but customers are encouraged to bring their own containers. All products can be tested on the premises. Started in 1905, the cider is produced with local apples. The cider is strong with good body and well made.

Reed's Cider
Broadhayes
Saw Mills
Stockland Near Honiton
Devon

Tel.: 0404 88366

Ciders Produced:
   Medium and Vintage

These ciders are available from the farm itself or in the Kings Arms in Stockland. Cider traditions are very strongly upheld here and the product is kept very well in the local pub. Highly recommended.

Redderways Farm Cider
Lower Rixdale
Luton
Ideford
Near Newton Abbott
Devon

Tel.: 0626 775218

Ciders Produced:
   Medium and Dry

Products are available to be sampled before purchasing. This is a subtle, local cider made in the most natural way. Stored in large oak barrels, the cider is clear and clean, with a very pleasant cinnamony after-taste.

Yearlstone Cider
Yearlstone Vinyard
Chilverton
Coldridge
Crediton
Devon

Tel.: 0363 83302

Ciders Produced:
  Gold, Vintage and Dry

All styles can be sampled before purchasing. The cider is made by Gillian Pearkes from locally grown apples, and the ciders are fermented in oak barrels. The Gold is a crisp, dry, elegant cider and is excellent with food. Care is taken to select only the best apples for the product.

SOMERSET

(Numbers relate to the map overleaf)

Brandy Producer
④ Royal Somerset Brandy

Beer Breweries
⑥ Ashvine Brewery
⑦ Berrow Brewery
② Bridgewater Brewing Co.
③ Cotleigh Brewey
⑤ Cottage Brewery
④ Exmoor Ales
① Royal Clarence Hotel

Cider Producers
Ash Hill Cider ⑥
Ashwood Cider ⑬
Art's Somerset Scrumpy ⑭
Avalon Cider ⑰
Brympton D'Evercy Cider ⑮
Burrow Hill Somerset Cider ⑦
Coombes Cider ①
Derrick's Cider ⑫
Lane's Cider ⑧
Perry's Farmhouse Cider ⑪
Rich's Farmhouse Cider ⑤
Roger Wilkins Farmhouse Cider ②
Rose's Cider ⑯
Sheppys Cider ⑩
W.E.Hecks & Son ③
Whitehead Cider ⑨

Somerset

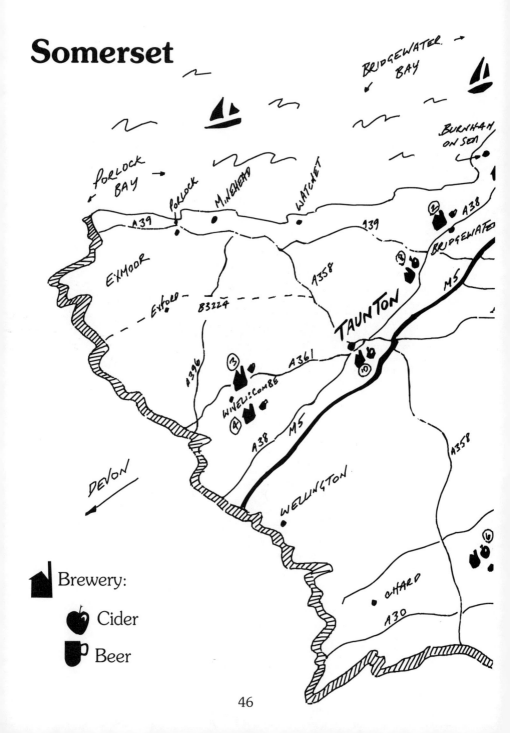

Brewery:

Cider

Beer

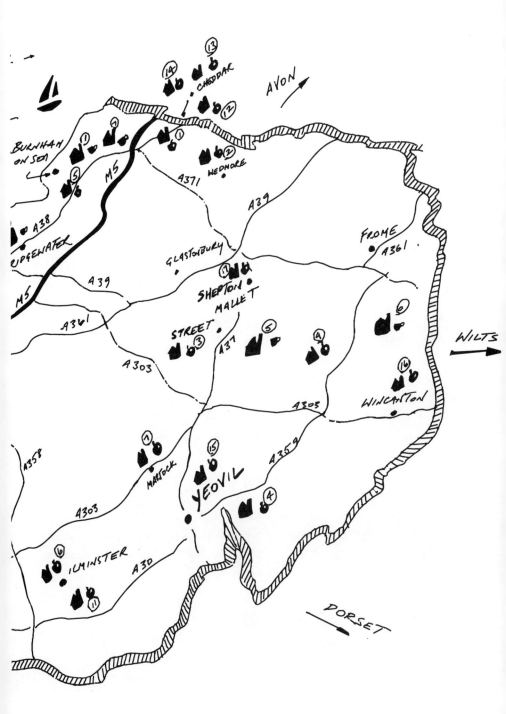

Royal Somerset Brandy
Pass Vale Farm
Burrow Hill
Brompton D'Evercy
Near Yeovil
Somerset

Tel.: 0460 40782

Cider brandy has not been distilled in this country for 700 years. At last a worthy product has been developed by Julian Temperley to take on the French Calvados. It was a struggle to obtain a license to distil apple brandy in the UK, but Julian is full of generous praise for the help and encouragement he received from French Calvados producers, and this spirit of cooperation has borne wonderful fruit. Royal Somerset Brandy is superb – subtle, smooth, appley with bags of flavour and a finish that goes on forever. It is highly recommended for anybody who enjoys brandy or calvados. The price is a snip at approximately £16 a bottle. It is available nationally in independent off-licences and now in certain Tesco supermarket chains, and Julian is happy for visitors to buy directly from the farm. Available at the moment is the three year old brandy. The five, ten and and fifteen-year-old Somerset brandies are gently resting in oak barrels at the Wickwaw Bond warehouse in Gloucestershire. Orders are being taken now, with the fifteen year old brandy available just in time to celebrate the new millennium, on 1st January 2000. Judging from the quality of the three year old, this should be stunning.

Rating:

BEERS

Ashvine Brewery
Whiteheart
Trudoxhill
Frome
Somerset

Tel.: 0373 836344

Beers Produced:	Original Gravity
Trudoxhill Bitter	**1034^0**
Ashvine Bitter	**1039^0**
Challenger	**1042^0**
Tanker	**1049^0**
Hope and Glory	**1058^0**

Originally set up in Taunton in 1987, the brewery moved to the Whiteheart in January 1989 and since then has bought a second tied house and supplies over fifty free trade outlets.

Trudoxhill Bitter is spicy, with golding hops. A malty medium dry finish with good long character. Well balanced.

Ashvine Bitter is a light gold brew with a floral hop aroma and fruity undertones. Powerful bitter and the hops dominate the taste. An unusual brew.

Challenger has delicate aromas of malt, and a full fruity mouth flavour. There is a slight acidity on the finish with a nutty fragrance. A ruby ale.

Tanker is a well developed, tawny bitter with fruity hops and a subtle sweetness on the finish. Slight aromas of honey.

Hope and Glory has a peppery, spicy nose with slight yeast coming through. A dark ale of a fruity dark flavour and a long malty finish.

Rating:

Berrow Brewery
Coast Road
Berrow
Burnham on Sea
Somerset

Tel.: 0278 751345

Beers Produced:	Original Gravity
Four B's	1038⁰
Topsy Turvey	1055⁰

Mrs. Johnston set up this little brewery with her husband ten years ago and since then she has been the main driving force behind the development of the increasingly renowned beers.

Four B's has a slight floral nose and malty hoppy palate, a pleasant fruity flavour and reasonable finish.

Topsey Turvey is a beer of powerful aromas of yeast and hops. It is well balanced, with a bitter finish.

Rating:

Bridgewater Brewing Company
Unit 1
Lovedere Farm
Goathurst
Bridgewater
Somerset

Tel.: 0278 663996

Beers produced:	Original Gravity
Amber	1040^0
Coppernob	1045^0
Sunbeam	1052^0

The Royal Oak near North Curry around 1900

51

Geoff Lucas started his brewery ten years ago and has built it into an excellent business.

Amber has a light hoppy nose and flavour with a fruity finish. Amber coloured and well made.

Coppernob is a richer but drier beer, with a full malty, yeasty flavour. Slightly nutty on the end. Darker coloured.

Sunbeam A sweeter honey flavoured beer with a sweet malty nose and a long lingering finish. The beer is light coloured, but full in flavour.

Rating:

Cotleigh Brewery
Ford Road
Witherliscombe
Somerset

Tel.: 0984 24086

Beers produced:	Original Gravity
Harrier SPA	1036^0
Nutcracker Mild	1036^0
Tawny Bitter	1040^0
Barn Owl Bitter	1048^0

Originally started in the Cotleigh Farmhouse in 1979, The brewery supplies almost a hundred outlets now. It has expanded hugely in the last two years.

Harrier SPA is a light coloured beer with a very hoppy and malty aroma. A bitter finish, but plenty of fruit flavours for a low gravity beer.

Nutcracker Mild is a beer of limited production, but a dark mild, lacking a certain finish.

Tawny Bitter is a flavoursome brown ale with huge amounts of fruit on the end of the palate. A lovely nutty and hoppy nose.

Barn Owl Bitter is a rich ale with chestnuts and coffee aromas. A chewy malt with a deep finish, dark ruby in colour.

Rating:

Cottage Brewery
Little Orchard
West Lydford
Somerset

Tel.: 0963 24383

Beers Produced:	Original Gravity
Somerset Dorset Railway	1037^0
Norman Conquest	1066^0

Chris Norman, now semi-retired from British Airways, has started up his own brewery producing some very worthy beers.

Somerset Dorset Railway Beer has a lovely smooth finish and very, very malty upfront start. Interesting nutty nose and long lasting flavour.

Norman Conquest is brewed limitedly, and has a full rich, nutty chocolaty finish.

Rating:

Exmoor Ales
Golden Hill Brewery
Witherliscombe
Somerset

Tel.: 0984 23798

Beers Produced:	Original Gravity
Exmoor Ale	1039⁰
Exmoor Gold	1045⁰
Exmoor Stag	1050⁰
Exmoor Beast	1066⁰

To quote their slogan, "We liked the beer so much, we bought the brewery". This is the true story of Jim Laker and Peter Turner, who worked for the brewery and decided to conduct a management buy out. Jim Laker is very active on behalf of SIBA, the Small Independent Brewers Association, promoting the cause of Britain's independent brewing industry with characteristic energy, aplomb – and a terrible line in puns! His brewery is an illustration of the "small is beautiful" principle – all his excellent beers are produced by traditional methods using West Country local malt and water.

The beers are widely distributed, but still keep the great flavour of independence.

Exmoor Ale is an award-winning bitter. A ripe, full, malty flavour with hops and citrus in the finish.

Exmoor Gold has a big woody and toffee nose. Great flavour of hops and fruits. Lovely, woody, golden ale with super aroma and strong finish.

Exmoor Stag is a fuller, richer beer with a floral hint. Its hard-hitting bitter taste mellows out to leave a voluptuous, malty finish. A great ale.

Exmoor Beast is a full, dark, porter-style beer, brewed in the winter months. A burnt but smooth flavour and a lovely, rich, complex aroma of chocolate, coffee and toffee. A worthy product with which to face the winter.

Rating:

Royal Clarence Hotel
Esplanade
Burnham on Sea
Somerset

Tel.: 0278 783138

Beers Produced: **Original Gravity**
   Clarence Pride   **1036⁰**

Old Slug Porter	**1045⁰**
Regent	**1050⁰**
Firebox	**1060⁰**

Ten years ago, the brewery was started as a sideline to the hotel. It is now so successful that it dominates this whole business. Not only do Paul Davies' beers satisfy his customers tastes at the hotel, but further afield too. He currently produces twenty barrels a week and hopes to expand further. He very much deserves his success.

Clarence Pride has a full, malty, dark-roasted nose with excellent balance on the mouth. A mouth-wateringly bitter finish with slight coffee tones. A dark malt character beer.

Old Slug Porter is made in a deliciously traditional style. Toffee and honey on the nose with full nutty and woody flavours. A lovely warmer.

Clarence Regent is another black winter brew with a dark brown flavour and an interesting herby, malty cinnamon palate.

Firebox is a high strength, creamy ale, with a velvet beginning and long toffeed finish. It is surprisingly smooth.

Rating:

CIDER

Art's Somerset Scrumpy
Lilypool Farm
Shipham
Cheddar
Somerset

Tel.: 0934 743994

Cider produced:
Somerset Scrumpy, Virgin's Ruin and Triple Vintage

Antique cider shoes used for warming cider in the fire

Run by Arthur David, the business is now closely linked to Broadoak Cider, where both products are available. The ciders are very well and traditionally made. A visit to the farm is interesting and recommended – there is also a farm shop selling apple juice and other local products.

Ash Hill Cider
Ashton Farms
Ash Hill
Near Illminster
Somerset

Tel.: 0823 480513

Cider produced:
Sweet and Dry

This is very much a traditional Somerset cider, terrifyingly strong, with a very pleasing flavour, despite just the two types on offer. The label says it all, perhaps – a girl kicking high with a glass of cider, and the inevitable punch line – "Cider with a real kick!" It is certainly well worth trying, and has been known to sell out, so do telephone to make sure of supplies.

Ashwood Cider
Shipham Hill
Cheddar
Somerset

Tel.: 0934 742393

Cider produced:
Sweet, Medium and Dry

A recent newcomer to cider production, the Fords started making cider in 1986. Nevertheless, the cider is made to traditional methods. The ciders are pleasant, with long-lasting flavour.

Harvesting apples to produce cider in 1908

Avalon Cider
Avalon Farm
The Drove
East Pennard
Shepton Mallet
Somerset

Tel.: 0749 86393

Cider Produced:
   Dry and Sparkling Dry

Not a cider to be drunk in the local pub by the pint! This is a more sophisticated blend, with a long-lasting flavour. Dr. Harold Tripp is proud of his cider, and rightly so. It is made from organic fruit, with no additives – the sparkling cider is a gem.

Brympton D'Evercy Cider
Brympton D'Evercy House
Yeovil
Somerset

Tel.: 0935 862528

Cider produced:
   Medium and Dry

The 750 year-old house itself is the main attraction, with of course the added bonus that cider is still produced on the farm. Only made of local Kingston Black apples, the cider is full of flavour and strength. A recommended visit is a half-day around the gardens, house and museum.

Burrow Hill Somerset Cider
Pass Vale Farm
Burrow Hill
Kingsbury Episcopi
Martock
Somerset

Tel.: 0460 40782

Cider produced:
Dry and Sweet

Traditional winter cider wassailing in the 1950s

This cider is well known locally. Julian Temperley, who makes it as a side product to his superb and unique Somerset Brandy, is something of a legend. He is very much a traditional cider maker who has won many awards, and as far as he is concerned, Somerset is the only county where good cider apples are grown. All his apples are locally grown – Porter's Perfection, Chisel Jersey, and Somerset Redstreak. Cider has been produced at Pass Vale Farm for over 100 years, matured in vast 10,000 gallon oak vats. His ciders are subtle, with interesting flavours, and well made from pure unconcentrated apple juice. All products can be sampled on site.

Coombes Cider
Japonica Farm
Mark
Near Highbridge
Somerset
TA9 4QD

Tel.: 0278 641265

Cider produced:
Dry, Medium and Sweet cider
Perry and Apple juice are also available

Chris Coombes has been producing his well-known ciders and perry in a family tradition which goes back over 100 years. His excellent, very mellow-tasting cider is made from the pure juice of his own or local cider apple and pear orchards. He will mix his ciders according to taste for you from his dry and sweet barrels. Also sold is sparking perry. The farm is popular with visitors and children, as there is a small cider museum and cider-making video available, as well as a children's play area. Highly recommended.

Derrick's Cider
Cheddar Valley
The Gorge
Cheddar
Somerset

Tel.: 0934 743113

Cider produced:
 **Tanglefoot medium sweet, Country Bumpkin sweet
 and Country Bumpkin dry**

All ciders can be sampled on site. Tony Derrick can be contacted to arrange visits or large party tastings. The famous Cheddar Gorge has an array of shops selling ciders, and of the selection on offer, Derrick's cider is definitely among the best. Do choose your time of year to visit, however – during the summer months the numbers of tourists visiting the area may strongly test your patience. Derrick's cider is well made, with an interesting flavour and a surprising fresh strength. Ciders can be sampled out of the original stone flagons in which they are stored.

Lane's Cider
Overton
West Monkton
Near Taunton
Somerset

Tel.: 0823 412345

Cider produced:
 Dry and Medium

A very modern cider-maker, using up to date technology, Gary Lane produces a worthy cider from Dabinett, Yarlington Mill and the famous Kingston Black apples. It is distributed locally to off-licenses, pubs and clubs in the Taunton area. Visits to this cider farm are recommended. You can bring your own gallon or half-gallon containers to be filled, or buy them on the spot.

An earthenware cider 'hedgehog' or 'owl'

Perry's Farmhouse Cider
Perry's Cider Mills
Dowlish Wake
Near Illminster
Somerset

Tel.: 04505 2681

Cider produced:
Medium sweet, Medium dry, Dry and Vintage

The Perry family have been making cider for many years. The cider is still produced in a lovely sixteenth century thatched barn, where the farming tools and equipment are authentically antique. The Perrys use cider apples from their own orchards, including: Bitter Yarlington Mill, Bulmer's Norman, Brown Snout, and Kingston Black. The ciders have an interesting flavour, and all vary considerably in style. They are well-made, with full appley flavours.

Rich's Farmhouse Cider
Cider Farm
Watchfield
Near Highbridge
Somerset
TA9 1ER

Tel.: 0278 783651

Rich's Cider Farm is another great experience for lovers of good, traditional cider. Mr. Rich and his daughter sell his excellent cider from huge wooden vats directly into whatever receptacle you happen to have brought: the steady stream of customers on the day I was there turned up with anything from bottles to milk churns for the day's supply. One group of connoisseurs hire a minibus and turn up regularly from the midlands, while on the walls of his barn are accolades from consumers further afield, including the women's wing of Pentonville Prison, the RAF and East German border guards!

Roger Wilkins Farmhouse Cider
Land's End Farm
Mudgeley
Wedmore
Somerset
BS28 4TU

Tel.: 0934 712385

Cider produced:
Dry and Sweet

At the end of a farm track in deepest Somerset, near Glastonbury, Roger Wilkins' farm is one of the last traditional cider farms in an area where only a few decades ago every farm produced scrumpy and cider for its labourers. He sells a potent, bone dry traditional cider (and a sweet cider) straight from the vats, and his "lounge bar" – a barn with six chairs – is a well-known Sunday watering hole for the discriminating locals. As the morning wears on the crowd swells and the chat becomes more philosophical, cheerfully abusive and even medicinal... women with overdue babies are advised to down a jar, with happy results guaranteed within twelve hours! Roger's cider is strongly recommended – you can bring your own containers, and either ask for directions in Wedmore or bring an Ordinance Survey map!

Rose's Cider
Rose Farm
Lattiford
Wincanton
Somerset

Tel.: 0963 33680

Cider produced:
Rose's dry

This cider is famous for its excellent quality. It is one of the best in Somerset. It is made only of local apples and has a most interesting flavour – initially sweet, with a dry nutty finish. The on-site shop is also worth visiting – more like a National Trust shop than the usual type of farm shop, and hung with the awards that Rose's cider has won in 1987 and 1988.

Sheppys Cider
Three Bridges
Bradford on Tone
Near Taunton
Somerset

Tel.: 0823 46233

Cider produced:
Farmhouse draught – sweet, medium, dry
Oakwood draught – sweet, medium, dry

The Sheppeys family has been producing cider for over 200 years. The cider has won many awards for its traditional and flavoursome style. A visit to the premises is encouraged and would make an interesting family day out. There is a cider museum and video on cider production, nature walks through the surrounding country-side, and a small farm shop with local products as well as cider – please telephone for opening hours. It is advisable to take your own cider containers.

The ciders are full-bodied, with a rounded flavour, and are very recommended.

W.E. Hecks and Son
9-11 Middle Leigh
Street
Somerset

Tel.: 0458 42367

Ciders produced:
    Sweet, Medium and Dry
    Several varieties of pure apple juice

John Hecks comes from a family of six generations of cider pro-ducers, since 1840. His award-winning sweet, medium and dry cider is made from the blended juices of his own and local cider apples. It is fermented in wooden barrels, producing a drink with a distinctive taste, and sold draught from the wood. Ten varieties of pure apple juice, including Kingston Black, are also available from the farm shop, as well as a selection of farm produce. On display at the farm is a well-preserved traditional cider press.

Traditional cider production – making a 'cheese' ready for pressing.

AVON

(Numbers relate to the map overleaf)

Beer Breweries
④ Butcombe Brewery Ltd.
② Hardington's Brewery
③ Hope and Anchor
⑥ Oakhill Brewery
⑤ The Ross Brewing Company
① Smiles Brewing Company Ltd.
⑦ Wickwar Brewing Company

Cider Producers
Broadoak Cider ③
Cowhill Cider ⑤
Long Ashton Cider ①
Rich's Cider ②
Thatchers Cider ④

Avon

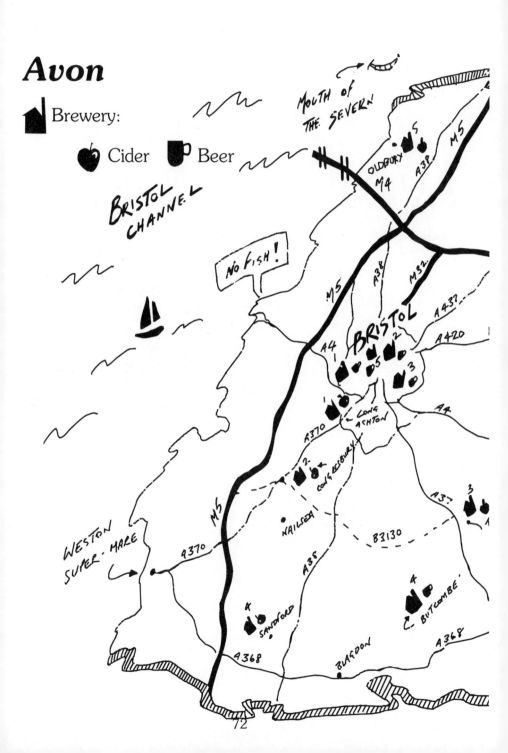

Brewery:

Cider   Beer

BRISTOL CHANNEL

MOUTH OF THE SEVERN

NO FISH!

OLDBURY

M4   A38   M5

M5   A38   M32

BRISTOL   A432   A420

A4

A4

LONG ASHTON   A4

A370

CONGRESBURY

NAILSEA   B3130

A37

WESTON SUPER-MARE   A370   A38

SANDFORD   C. BUTCOMBE   A368

A368   BLAGDON   A368

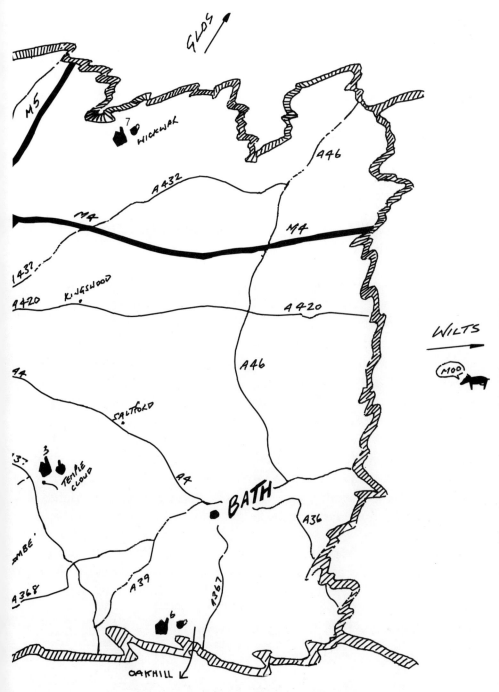

BEERS

Butcombe Brewery Ltd.
Butcombe
Near Bristol
Avon

Tel.: 0275 472240

Beer produced:	Original Gravity
Butcombe Bitter	**1039^0**

Simon Whitmore started Butcombe Brewery in 1978, with a pedigree before him of managing director of Courage Weston, marketing director of Guinness in Malaysia and general manager for Courage in Australia. He originally started with a staff of three, and has now expanded to eight staff, producing over 200 barrels a week. There were initial problems in obtaining planning permission for the brewery, but he eventually convinced the Planning Committee with the excuse that producing beer is a rural craft. Unfortunately, visits to the brewery are not possible, because the staff's busy working day cannot extend to supervising visitors. The brewery and staff have very much a family feel – in fact every night the eight of them get together and play spoof, to work out which duties are assigned to whom the next day.

The beer is very popular in the West Country, although Simon himself, a perfectionist, is still looking to improve the product. It is widely available, but especially around Butcombe. It has a lovely floral aroma, with a long hoppy nose. The taste is very refreshing, with a dry brewing finish and interesting fruit flavours. A well made beer.

Rating:

Hardington's Brewery
Albany Buildings
Dean Lane
Bristol
Avon

Tel.: 0272 636194

Beers produced:	Original Gravity
Traditional Bitter	1038^0
Best Bitter	1042^0
Jubilee	1050^0
Moonshine	1050^0
Old Lucifer	1050^0

The brewery began in April 1991, and now supplies up to 40 outlets in Bristol, Somerset and Avon. They own their own pub, **The Swan with Two Necks**, in St. Judes, Bristol, which is well worth a visit. The quality of the beers is always consistant -this is certainly a brewery to watch for the future.

Traditional Bitter has an interesting floral nose, with a full hop and citrus finish. On the palate is has a keen taste, a little sweetness in the middle, with a very well balanced malt and yeasty finish.

Best Bitter is a crisp, amber beer with a bitter-sweet finish, and a long-lasting dry, floral, hoppy start. Malt dominates on the nose.

Jubilee is a complex, warming beer, with full hops and spice on the nose. Rich and dark in the mouth, and a complex fruity, sultana finish.

Moonshine has a strong barley smell, with a similiar citrus nose on the end. The beer is smooth and slightly sweet in flavour with a spicy finish.

Old Lucifer is very smooth for the strength, has a very hoppy aroma, with a powerful, bitter-sweet start, warm in the middle, with a complex hoppy end. A great beer.

Rating:

Hope and Anchor
Jacobs Wells Road
Hotwells
Bristol
Avon

Tel.: 0272 292987

Beers produced:	Original Gravity
Jack High	1038°
Eight Barrels Special	1050°
O'Hooligan Stout	1050°

The most recently set-up brewery-pub in the book, it was started by Steve Simpson-Wells in November 1993. He is a perfectionist to the end. So far, the products are excellent – although Steve is always seeking to improve upon them. Steve started making beer as a hobby in the Penarth Hotel in Wales before coming to Bristol, and has never had experience with any other brewery. Despite this, his products are excellent and worth trying.

We hope by July 1994 to see the launch of a new product – Lucifer lager. My reason for mentioning this is because it will be unique: a live, cask-conditioned lager, the first to be produced in the UK. The pub is unspoilt, and although not yet complete is open to the public, and has a nice, cosy atmosphere. I wish Steve the best of luck for the future, and am sure his products will spread across the West Country and eventually nationally. This is definately a brewery to watch.

Jack High is a light, refreshing, amber-coloured ale ale, with a pleasant, yeasty aroma, and a slight hint of citrus on the end of the nose. On the palate, it is dry, long and refreshing. A velvety texture, with great balance. Marvellously made.

Eight Barrels Special is a big beer. On the nose, it has a voluptuous, velvety start, lingering hops and malt, ending with a nutty aroma. It is a full, yeasty, fruity beer on the palate, with a slight burnt taste. Hazelnuts dominate on the finish, which is also slightly toffeed.

O'Hooligan Stout is, to my mind, the perfect stout – a massively long-lasting flavour, with a voluptuous toffee and honeyed nose. It has slightly burnt yeast flavours on the fore-front, leading into a lingering creamy taste. Excellent bitter balance of acidity, and extremely well made.

Rating:

Oakhill Brewery
Old Brewery
High Street
Oakhill
Bath
Avon

Tel.: 0747 840134

Beers produced:	Original Gravity
Oakhill Bitter	1044^0
Black Magic Stout	1044^0
Yeomans Strong Ale	1049^0

Situated on the original Oakhill Brewery site, established 1767, the Oakhill Brewery was set up in 1984 by local farmer Reg Keevil. Recently the brewing has been done by John Lawton, whose background is with the David Bruce – Firkin pubs.

Oakhill Bitter is amber coloured with a malty aroma, hoppy and bitter in the mouth with good balancing and acidity. It has a good strong finish.

Black Magic Stout has a bitterish toffee and coffee nose with a dark malt and toasted grain in the mouth flavour. It is a full stout beer.

Yeoman's Strong Ale is a beer with an interesting bitter sweet finish, a powerful nose and rich copper colour.

Rating:

The Ross Brewing Company's popular bottled organic beer – Saxon

The Ross Brewing Company
The Bristol Brew House
117 Stokes Croft
Bristol
Avon

Tel.: 0272 428746

Beers produced:	Original Gravity
Clifton Dark	1045⁰
Hartcliffe Bitter	1045⁰
Kingsdowner	1045⁰
Medieval Porter	1045⁰

Set up in 1989, the Ross Brewery became famous for being the first brewery to use Organic Association barley. The brewery originally produced a range of bottle-conditioned beers only, until the acquisition of the Bristol Brewhouse pub, where they produce cask-conditioned ales, and one remaining bottle-conditioned ale, Saxon Strong. Production is mainly for the Brew pub, although they do supply to a limited number of free trade outlets.

Clifton Dark ale has a strong malty nose, with hints of fruit at the end. On the palate, a rich toffee and caramel malt flavour, with a lingering bitter-sweet finish.

Hartcliffe Bitter is a pale brown malty beer, with a lingering sweetish nose. On the palate, a full, dominating hops flavour, with a fruity end.

Kingsdowner is an occasionally brewed beer – unfortunately I've yet to have the chance to try it!

The most well known beer logo in Bristol – Smiles Best

Medieval Porter is an unusually copper-coloured brown porter, with a roast malt aroma, and slight traces of herbs on the finish. The taste is full, dry and spicy, with a bitter-sweet end. Slight hints of ginger at the beginning, with a long, complex flavour.

Rating:

Smiles Brewing Company Limited
Colston Yard
Colston Street
Bristol
Avon

Tel.: 0272 297350

Beers produced:	Original Gravity
Brewery Bitter	1037⁰
Best Bitter	1041⁰
Exhibition	1051⁰
Bristol Stout	1046⁰

Started in 1977 to supply local restaurants and pubs, Smiles has now expanded into one of the largest independents in the region. They have won various CAMRA awards, including 1990 Best Pub refurbishment and 1991 Best Pub Award – by their pub next door to the brewery, The Brewery Tap. Another Smiles pub I recommended is the – as yet – completely unspoiled, no frills, horse brasses or carpets – Highbury Vaults at the top of St. Michael's Hill, Cotham, Bristol. The interior is cosy and there is a very pleasant leafy and partly covered courtyard at the back where children are welcome. The Highbury keeps its beer very well, and always has a variety of guest beers and ciders in addition to the Smiles' range. There have been, however, recent dire rumours of a new accountant's suggestion that a television and a juke box might increase the bottom line... as the pub is always packed full of people who come precisely to get away from pub juke boxes, we hope this brilliant notion will die a natural death!

Smiles have five managed pubs and supply 200 free trade outlets, and are still searching out more tied houses. They are a brewery of modern outlook and produce beers of excellent quality. The Smiles truck can often be seen being driven around Bristol by one of the original founding partners! Smiles has a high profile in Bristol and is widely available in the South West.

Brewery Bitter is an amber light ale, with plenty of malt on the nose, and a large hoppy flavour on the palate. A fruity beer, with a pleasant, slightly nutty finish.

Best Bitter is deliciously delicate, has a malty bouquet, with slight yeast hints on the end. In the mouth, slightly sweet, but deliciously long flavour with a dry and balanced end. In the middle, nuts, hops and slightly toffeed. Very well made.

Exhibition Bitter is a deep copper-coloured beer, with a complex nose, consisting of malt, hops, yeast, toffee and citrus fruits. On the mouth it has a full, dry, lingering flavour, well balanced and complex, considering the strength. A very well made beer.

Bristol Stout is only available in the winter. A full, roasted nut and stout aroma, slightly toffeed on the end. A malty palate, with a full, hoppy, bitter finish.

Rating:

Wickwar Brewing Company
The Old Cider Mill
Station Road
Wickwar
Avon

Tel.: 0454 294168

Beers produced: / **Original Gravity**
- Coopers — 1036⁰
- Brand Oak Bitter — 1039⁰
- Olde Merryford Ale — 1049⁰
- Station Porter — 1060⁰

Brian Rydes and Ray Penny, both old Courage tenants, opened this brewery in May of 1990 and today production has risen to approximately sixty barrels a week. The site is on the original Arnold Perrett brewery, for 300 years one of the most famous breweries in the region. It closed 30 years ago and now the Wickwar brewery has revived the venerable tradition. Their beers are now available in over fifty free-trade outlets.

Coopers Ale has a golden amber hue, producing a refreshing, hoppy nose. On the palate the beer is very delicate, with lime and oranges on the forefront, with a slight sweet maltiness in the middle and a complex, dry bitter finish.

Brand Oak Bitter has a full, malty, fruit nose. On the palate, a rich, powerful flavour of hops, slightly yeasty up front, with a long, lingering, bitter-sweet nutty finish. Brand oak Bitter is affectionately known as BOB throughout the West Country.

Olde Merryford Ale is a pale bitter, but full-flavoured, with a long, yeasty, hoppy nose, slightly sweet up front, and a very long lasting taste of citrus, malt, hops and yeast with a hint of toffee and a slight trace of wood on the finish. It is very dry.

Station Porter is a very smooth-style porter, ending with a long, lingering, bitter-sweet finish. A strong porter, with a rich coffee nose and full fruit aroma. Very complex and yeasty in the middle. Very much an old-style porter, and highly recommended.

Rating:

CIDERS

Broadoak Cider
Clutton
Near Temple Cloud
Avon

Tel.: 0761 453119

The Broadooak Vintage bottled cider label

Ciders prodcued:
   Broadoak Dry, Medium, Moonshine
   and Vintage –
      Dry, medium dry, medium and sweet

Broadoak produces a range of traditional ciders of some finesse. They are now in full production, and bottle some of their range. The ciders have an old, up-front taste of traditional character. Particularly recommended is Broadoak Moonshine, which is an 8% clear white cider of an exceptional applely flavour. Broadoak dry is of a refreshing, crisp and fruity flavour, perfect for the summer. The vintage range is full of flavour and well matured.

Cow Hill Cider
Fisherman's Cottage
Cow Hill
Oldbury on Severn
Near Thornbury
Avon

Tel.: 0454 412152

Cider produced:
   Dry, Medium and Medium sweet.

For traditional cider you need look no further. The press used here is of a kind normally found in cider museums! Cow Hill Cider is run by John Tymko. Nothing has changed production methods for decades, and he uses apples from his own orchards. The ciders are fruity and light, and very popular locally. John is a great cider maker, but he admits that most of the work is done by nature. The ciders are strongly recommended, and the farm well worth visiting, although it is advisable to phone first.

Long Ashton Cider
Long Ashton Research Station
Long Ashton
Near Bristol
Avon

Tel.: 0272 392181

Ciders produced:
Medium sweet, Medium dry, Dry and Sparkling medium sweet ciders and "champagne-style" Perry

The Long Ashton Research station was formed in 1903, and was absorbed by 1912 into Bristol University. The plant itself is interesting to visit – it is advisable to contact Martin Gibson to arrange a visit. As well as producing their own ciders, they used to act as an advisory committee on cider manufacturing but now specialize in agriculture. Their production system is very advanced, although the ciders are naturally made, with good levels of acidity. The ciders are not pasteurized, so there is no unpleasant after-taste – nor are they filtered. All have a slightly woody flavour.

Rich's Cider
The Corner Cottage
Congresbury
Bristol
Avon

Tel.: 0934 832054

Cider produced:
Sweet, Medium and Dry

Cider is produced at Rich's mainly for the Bristol market, and for the summer tourist market. It is very popular in the area. the ciders are well made, strong and fruity – and excellent value for money.

Thatchers Cider
Myrtle Farm
Station Road
Sandford
Avon

Tel.: 0934 822862

Cider produced:
Sweet, Medium, Mendip Magic and
Sandford's Superb –
Sweet, Medium and Dry

The farm started producing cider in 1903, but expanded dramatically in 1982 in the Cheddar valley. The production is large, and despite this an impressive one third of the apples used are home-grown. This is very much a traditional, scrumpy-style cider, cloudy and unfiltered. There is a carbonated brand called **Mendip Magic**. Distribution is across the West Country, and to pubs from Hampshire to Kent.

WILTSHIRE

(Numbers relate to the map opposite)

Beer Breweries

⑦ Archer Ales Ltd.

⑩ Arkils Brewery

⑥ Bunce's Brewery

⑨ Foxely Brewing Company

② Gibb's New Brewery

① The Hop Back Brewery

⑧ Mole's Brewery

④ Ushers of Trowbridge

⑤ Wadworth and Co. Ltd.

Cider Producer

The Sellers Cider Co. ③

Wiltshire

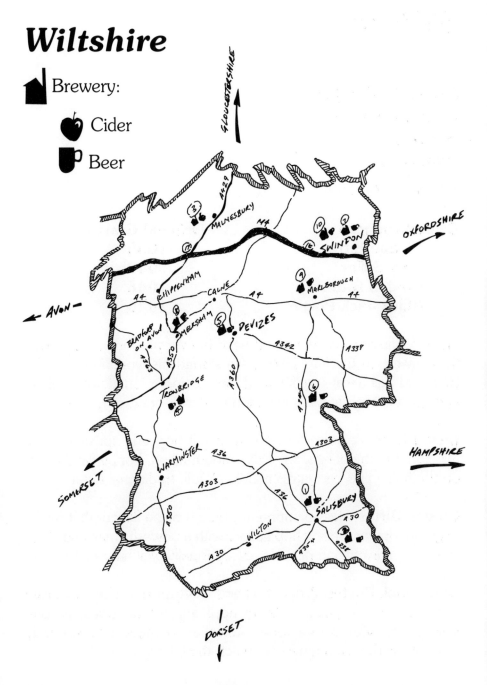

Brewery:

Cider

Beer

GLOUCESTERSHIRE

OXFORDSHIRE

A429

MALMESBURY

M4

10 7

16 SWINFON

9

MARLBOROUGH

CHIPPENHAM

CALNE

A4

A4

AVON

A4

BRADFORD ON AVON

A365

MELKSHAM

A350

DEVIZES

5

A342

A338

A360

A361

6

TROWBRIDGE

WARMINSTER

A36

A303

A350

SOMERSET

A303

A36

A30

WILTON

A30

1

SALISBURY

A30

A3094

A338

HAMPSHIRE

DORSET

BEERS

Archers Ales Ltd.
London Street
Swindon
Wiltshire

Tel.: 0793 896789

Beers Produced:	Original Gravity
Village Bitter	1035⁰
Best Bitter	1040⁰
Golden Bitter	1046⁰
Black Jack Porter	1046⁰

Mark Wallingford is owner and head brewer and originally started the brewery in the late 1970s. He started his working life in the RAF and has always maintained that "being a fanatic of drinking and sport is a perfect combination to start a brewery....".

Best Bitter: A powerful nose with full hop and spices coming through. On the palate, an acidic, mouth-filling, hoppy flavour, dry on the finish and part citrus middle. A full, traditional bitter.

Golden Bitter: Has an impressive mouth-filling flavour that seems to go on forever. Strong hop flavour with a powerful malt and citrus aroma. A very strong pale ale, exceptionally well-balanced.

Black Jack Porter: A dark fruit and malty aroma. The immediate sensation on the palate is burnt hops and a bitter-sweet flavour. Very fruity with coffee tones. Excellently made and superbly balanced with a creaminess to match the bitterness.

Rating:

Arkils Brewery
Kingsdown Brewery
Upper Stratton
Swindon
Wiltshire

Tel.: 0793 823026

Beers Produced:	Original Gravity
2B	1032^0
Mash Tun Mild	1036^0
3B	1040^0
Kingsdown Ale	1052^0
Noel Ale	1055^0

Started in 1843, the brewery is still a family-owned business, with James Arkil as managing director. They have a distribution of 82 tied pubs and 160 free-trade outlets can be found all over the South West. This is a brewery steeped in tradition, using traditional methods to make real cask-conditioned bitters.

2B: A very well-bodied ale with a bitter finish and a full fruit and honeyed start. A refreshing beer with great balance.

Mash Tun Mild: A fresh, full, smooth, hoppy nose. A dark malty mouth on the palate with a creamy fresh finish. Slightly nutty and chocolaty. Very fine, dark, delicious malt.

3B: Darkish bitter giving a nutty flavour and interesting honeyed nose. A long finish which, at the end, is slightly too bitter.

Kingsdown Ale is a very strong, tawny ale with a rich hoppy aroma ending with a bitter-sweet finish. Slightly nutty.

Noel Ale: Produced for Christmas, it has a very sweet nose with a powerful, long hoppy flavour and a deep, bitter-sweet finish. A golden beer, very well balanced.

Rating:

Bunce's Brewery
The Old Mill
Mill Lane
Nether Avon
Wiltshire

Tel.: 0980 70631

Beers Produced:	Original Gravity
Bench Mark	1035°
Pigswill	1040°
Best Bitter	1042°
Old Smokey	1050°

Bunce's was purchased in the last couple of years by Stick Anderson, a Dane with brewing experience from "probably the largest brewery in Denmark..." In his own words, he describes Danish beer as "tasteless, cheap lager", which is the reason he came to the UK to produce traditional English ale, and he does it very well.

Benchmark: A bitter with a fruity nose and a full malty, mouth-filling flavour. Not rich, but a very refreshing beer.

Pigswill: Very warming, pleasant, voluptuous malty and hoppy nose. A full-balanced flavour, ending with a bitter finish.

Best Bitter is a golden ale with a flowery nose. It is slightly too fruity and acidic on the palate for my taste, but with lots of hops to finish.

Old Smokey: On the nose it lives up to its name. Spicy and a slightly smokey, woody finish. On the palate, a dark thick beer with a rounded, bitter-sweet finish and full fruit in the middle. Slightly toffeed. Well worth a try.

Rating:

Foxley Brewing Company
Unit 3
Home Farm Workshops
Mildenhall
Malborough
Wiltshire

Tel.: 0672 515000

Beers Produced:	Original Gravity
Foxley Best Bitter	1038^0
Dogporter Strong Ale	1048^0

95

The brewery was started in 1992 by Rob Owen and Neil Collins. They say themselves that their brewing experience comes from trial and error and they now think they've got it right. I tend to agree. The beer has a distribution of an approximately 60 mile radius around Marlborough and locally is much respected.

Foxley Best Bitter has a light hop and malty aroma. On the palate it starts off with an interesting nutty flavour and goes into a smooth yeasty and light-style bitter. Amber in colour.

Dogporter Strong Ale has a more seeded nose with full malty and hop aromas. On the palate it's long and complex with an interesting, honeyed end.

Rating:

Gibb's Mew Brewery
Anchor Brewery
Milford Street
Salisbury
Wiltshire

Tel.: 0722 411911

Beers Produced:	Original Gravity
Wiltshire Traditional Bitter	1036°
Timothy Chudley's Local Line	1036°
Premium Bitter	1042°
Salisbury Best Bitter	1042°
Bishop's Tipple	1066°

Gibb's Mew PLC was made very famous over the last few years by the renowned beer "Bishop's Tipple" which won the 1992 Champion Beer of Britain competition, now available in bottle nationally. This working brewery is well worth a visit, but please phone first for an appointment. The majority of ales are available in local pubs in Salisbury.

Wiltshire Traditional Bitter is a fresh, fruity, hoppy beer. Very well balanced and a light, easy-drinking tipple.

The **Timothy Chudley's Local Line** is very similar to Wiltshire Traditional Bitter. Slightly drier and not quite as fruity.

A far fruitier beer is the **Premium Bitter**, slightly sweet in the mouth with a long, malty finish.

Salisbury Best Bitter has a big, full, fruity nose with a flavour fully filling the mouth. Sweet, very hoppy, slightly fruity. Very enjoyable.

An 80 year old farm worker and very regular drinker! — from an advertising brochure of 1908

97

The **Bishop's Tipple** is the brewery's strongest beer (6.5% alcohol by volume), dry first of all, but very earthy with a slight toffee finish. Very malty in the mouth, deep, with hints of chocolate. Great beer.

Rating:

The Hop Back Brewery
27 East Court Road
Salisbury
Wiltshire
SP1 3A3

Tel.: 0722 328594

Beers Produced:	Original Gravity
Mild	1032^0
G.F.B.	1035^0
Special	1041^0
Wilt Alternative	1042^0
Entire Stout	1043^0
Summer Lightning	1050^0
Wheat Beer	1051^0

The brewery was started six years ago, run from the Wyndham Arms pub in Salisbury. John Gilbert and Roddy McBride started the brewery together, combining experience from Watneys and the Royal Tunbrige Wells Brewery. Success has been quick for them both, having achieved the Best Strong Beer in the Great British Beer Festival in 1992 for their Summer Lightning. A visit is highly recommended as the beers are wonderful and they have won many awards since.

The **Mild** has an exceptional hoppy character. It is a dark malt with a very hoppy aroma. On the palate, it has a rich toast flavour in the mouth and a very, very smooth finish, ending with a hint of vanilla.

G.F.B. is a golden amber coloured ale with a woody, oaky taste and with a bitter, dry finish. A wonderful pale ale.

The **Special** has a voluptuous malty and nutty aroma, with smooth hops filling the mouth. A very, very long finish. Creamy and delicious beer.

Wiltshire Alternative is a refreshing beer, although quite strong. It starts with a peppery nose, and is dry in the mouth. Long tasting fruits come through on the end.

Entire Stout is recognisable by its big, chocolaty nose with a sweeter palate but the usual full hops flavour. Very long on the finish, ending with hints of coffee and liquorice. A dry bitter.

Summer Lightning is a wonderful beer, with huge aromas of hops, intensely fruity on the palate with slight citrus undertones. A pale bitter, but superbly made.

Lastly the **Wheat Beer** is perhaps the most interesting product of all – it has a powerful herby nose and a very herby flavour on the palate. Lots of malt and hops are present. A pale bitter, very, very refreshing.

Overall Rating: 🍺🍺🍺🍺🍺

Mole's Brewery
5 Merlin Way
Bowerhill
Melksham
Wiltshire

Tel.: 0225 708842

Beers Produced:	Original Gravity
Best Bitter	1040^0
Mole's Brew 97	1050^0
XB	1060^0

Owned and run by Roger Catte, the brewery was started up approximately eleven years ago, and produces around 50 barrels a week. Mole's own a small chain of about eleven of their own pubs. Roger Catte is a strong critic of the large breweries and his brewery is well worth visiting.

The **Best Bitter** is a well made, hoppy bitter with a light malty nose and a long lasting bitter-sweet hoppy flavour. Slightly nutty on the finish.

For a riper aroma there is the **Mole's Brew 97** which has a very strong malty taste and slight ginger hints. A well balanced, complex beer full of hops and fruit, slightly red in colour.

The **XB** is a straightforward, strong ale, slightly lacking in fruit flavour, but a nice beer with a complex end.

Rating:

Ushers of Trowbridge
Directors House
68 Fore Street
Trowbrige
Wiltshire

Tel.: 0225 763171

Beers Produced:	Original Gravity
Usher's Best Bitter	1037⁰
Ushers Founders Ale	1045⁰
1824 Particular	1060⁰

Originally founded in 1824, Ushers lost its independence when it was swallowed up by Watneys in 1960. Thank goodness for a management buy out in 1992 which has made this great brewery independent. It now runs approximately thirty of its own pubs.

Ushers Best has a spicy, hoppy aroma with a malty, mouth filling flavour. Although the beer is sometimes variable, if it is kept well it's good.

The **Founders Ale** is a richer, more hoppy beer with a fruity nose. Slightly lemony in the mouth, with full fruity flavours. A dark amber colour with a very bitter finish.

1824 Particular is a strong and powerful winter ale with a rich fruity nose and rich tasting malts on the palate. Nutty and chocolaty but very well balanced. Slightly bitter-sweet on the finish.

Rating:

Wadworth and Co. Ltd.
Northgate Brewery
Devizes
Wiltshire

Tel.: 0380 723361

Beers Produced:	Original Gravity
Henry Wadsworth IPA	1034^0
6X	1040^0
Farmers Glory	1046^0
Old Timer	1055^0

Originally set up in 1885 by Henry Wadsworth and still holds to many of his traditional production methods, and even maintains the horse-drawn drays around the village of Devizes. They produce over 2000 barrels a week to supply pubs all over the south of England, including 190 tied houses. The famous beer at this brewery is the 6X.

Henry Wadsworth IPA has a very floral and hoppy nose with a big, mouth filling malty flavour. Slightly dry on the finish but very well balanced and a lovely, refreshing biscuity bitter.

A full bodied and distinctive bitter, **6X**, has an earthy hoppy nose and slightly nutty on the finish. A complex beer with mouth filling, long, malty flavours, and slightly vanilla. Copper coloured, enormously deep and complex.

Farmer's Glory is a delightfully fruity, hoppy beer with floral flavours. the nose is dryish and it finishes with a slightly toffeed finesse.

The strong **Old Timer** bitter has a wonderful fruity, hoppy aroma.

Butterscotch predominates but it is still fresh and bitter on the finish. A classically well made beer, also available in the bottle.

Rating:

CIDER

The Sellers Cider
Sherston Earl Vineyards Ltd.
Sherston
Malmsbury
Wiltshire

Tel.: 0666 840716

Ciders produced:
Sellers Dry, Sherston Scorcher (medium) and
Sellers Cider (medium sweet)

Sellers Cider is the only producer I have come across so far in Wiltshire that I want to include here. It is run by Norman Sellers. The ciders are very strong, some of them approaching wine strength, so beware if driving (or even walking!) The majority of styles are single apple varieties. To try the ciders, you'll have to visit the premises. If you're thinking of going along after normal retail times, please phone first, though Norman is very obliging and happy to see customers at any time.

*A woodcut from one of the first publications concerning cider –
'Vinetum Britannicum' 1678*

DORSET

(Numbers relate to the map overleaf)

Beer Breweries

③ Cook's Brewery Company
⑥ Elridge Pope
⑤ Goldfinch Brewery
① Hall and Woodhouse Ltd.
④ Palmers Ltd.
② The Poole Brewery

Dorset

Brewery:

Cider

Beer

Dorset

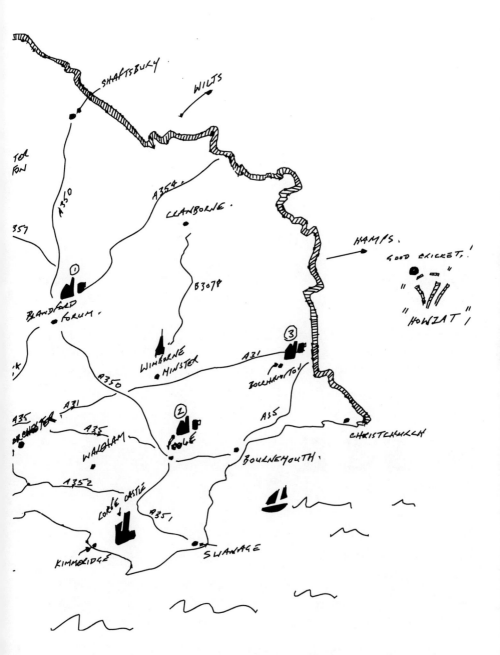

109

BEERS

Cook's Brewery Company
44 Burleigh Road
Bockhampton
Near Christchurch
Dorset

Tel.: 0425 73721

Beer Produced: **Original Gravity**
   Yard Arm Special Bitter   **1051⁰**

Production at this brewery started in May 1991, although Nigel Cook himself has got at least eighteen years of experience.

Yard Arm Special Bitter is a rich, nutty and malty nose, finishing with tinges of spice. In the mouth, a rounded malt flavour with a deep crisp finish. Slight ending of chocolate and toffee and hops. A rich aromatic ale, very well balanced and well made.

Rating:

Elridge Pope & Co.
Weymouth Avenue
Dorchester
Dorset

Tel.: 0305 251251

Beers Produced:	Original Gravity
Dorchester Bitter	1032^0
Best Bitter	1036^0
Blackdown Fort Porter	1040^0
Thomas Hardy Country Bitter	1040^0
Royal Oak	1048^0

Started in 1880, Eldridge Pope has been successfully brewing beer for over 100 years. Until recently it was independent, but the wholesale and free trade business was bought out last year by Carlsberg-Tetley, which may possibly have affected the beer. The company now seems aloof and unwilling to chat to customers and trade alike. Despite this, I soldiered on to try the beers impartially!

Dorchester Bitter is a light beer with a slight hoppy nose, reasonably balanced.

Best Bitter has a mixture of high malt and a hoppy nose, with a slight hint of fruit on the palate. Bland, with no after-taste.

Blackdown Fort Porter: An interesting porter with a light finish. On the nose, coffee and chocolate and a slightly blackcurranty taste.

Thomas Hardy Country Bitter: The overriding factor with this beer is the very, very bitter finish. Dry and hoppy on the nose with slight undertones of fruit at the beginning, but the bitter end goes on forever.

Royal Oak is a full-bodied beer with a full, fruity tropical flavour on the palate. Slightly sweet on the nose, but well-balanced.

Rating:

Goldfinch Brewery
(Tom Brown's Public House)
47 High East Street
Dorchester
Dorset

Tel.: 0305 264020

Beers Produced: **Original Gravity**
   Tom Brown's Best Bitter 1039^0
   Flashman's Clout Strong Ale 1043^0
   Midnight Blinder 1050^0

A good brewery/pub set in the middle of Dorchester. The pub itself, Tom Brown's Public House, has a theme based on the original book, and the beers are well kept and well served. The brewery was established in 1987.

Tom Brown's Best Bitter is a pale bitter with a fruity and malty nose. A bitter-sweet taste with lots of yeast and fruit, blending into a long, bitter finish.

Flashman's Clout Strong Ale has a honeyed, sweet nose, yet is bitter on the taste. Some strong hoppy flavours with a long, malty and yeasty finish.

Midnight Blinder has a full, rich, malty nose and a rich malty mouth too. A powerful, bitter finish. A complex beer, very well made.

Rating:

Hall and Woodhouse Ltd.
The Brewery
Blandford Forum
Dorset

Tel.: 0258 452141

Beers Produced:	Original Gravity
Coopers WPA	1036⁰
Badger's Best Bitter	1041⁰
Tanglefoot	1048⁰

Hall and Woodhouse are commonly known as "Badger's Brewery". Originally formed in 1777, they are still independent. The brewery serves one hundred and forty pubs in the local area and five hundred free-trade outlets.

Badger's Best Bitter is a great best bitter with a strong hoppy nose and on the palate, malty and fruity. A hoppy finish that goes on forever. Very well balanced.

The **Coopers WPA** is both flowery and citrusy on the nose with strong hops that dominate the palate, ending with a dry bitter flavour.

The strongest beer, **Tanglefoot**, is surprisingly pale in colour with a big, powerful, hoppy flavour. Overall it is smooth and palatable with a bitter-sweet end. The beer is deceptively alcoholic for the taste.

Rating:

Palmers Ltd.
The Old Brewery
West Bay Road
Bridport
Dorset

Tel.: 0308 422396

Beers produced:	Original Gravity
Bridport Bitter	1031^0
Palmers Best Bitter	1039^0
Tallyho	1046^0

Situated right on the coast at Bridport, Palmers is Britain's only thatched brewery. The brewery is still owned by the Palmer family, although it was started 200 years ago. Although the Palmer family is related to the Elridge Pope family (see page 110), when it comes to the quality of the beer, there's no comparison. Palmers have an efficient distribution throughout the South West area and seem to be expanding on a yearly basis.

Bridport Bitter has a delicate, nutty aroma with light hops and yeast. On the palate, a full, hoppy flavour with a clean and fresh finish. Well-balanced. A good bitter.

Palmers Best Bitter has superb. strong, malty aroma and huge, mouth-filling, malty taste. Finely balanced, with a fruity and nutty finish.

Tallyho is a dark and complex beer with a full nutty nose and nuts on the finish. Slightly sweet in the beginning but a long and complex fruity end. A strong, dark beer, made with little sugar giving a full bitter flavour. Very well balanced.

Rating:

The Poole Brewery
Brewhouse Brewery
68 High Street
Poole
Dorset

Tel.: 0202 682345

Beers Produced:	Original Gravity
Dolphin Bitter	1038^0
Bosun's Best Bitter	1045^0

The Poole Brewery was established in 1981 and then in 1990 the pub/brewhouse was completed. For a small brewery, the operation is successful and highly technical, using up-to-date methods to produce cask-conditioned beers.

Dolphin Bitter has a herby, spicey nose with a strong hoppy aroma. On the palate it is finely balanced, with hops in the mouth and a long lingering finish which is slightly nutty. A refreshing beer.

Bosun's Best Bitter has a yeastier, creamier nose, with a slight tartness at the end. On the palate, it is mellow with a full, ripe, hoppy balanced flavour and intensely bitter. Very well balanced.

Rating:

The seasoned beer and cider drinker always knows when they've had enough

INDEX

(Page numbers in bold type relate to specific drinks)

B

D

J

Jack High **77**
Janners Ale **26**
Janners Christmas Ale **26**
Janners Old Original **26**
Johnston, Mrs. 50
Jubilee **76**

K

Kings Arms, The 41
Kings Bitter **21**
Kingsdown Ale **94**
Kingsdowner **80**
Kingston Black apples 15, 60, 64, 65, 68
Kingston Black Cider apples 12

L

Laker, Jim 54
Lane, Gary 64
Lane's Cider **63–64**
Lawton, John 78
Legend Bitter **11**
liqueur 4–5
London Inn, The 10
Long Ashton Cider **87**
Long Ashton Research Station 87
Lost Withiel 14, 15
Lucas, Geoff 52
Lucifer lager **77**
Luscombe Cider **40**
Luxton, Graham 22

M

Malborough 95
Malpin, Mr. and Mrs. 39
Martock 61
Mash Tun Mild **93**
McBride, Roddy 98
McCraig, David 27

Royal Somerset Brandy **48–49**
Royal Tunbrige Wells Brewery 98
Rydes, Brian 83

S

Salisbury 96, 98
Salisbury Best Bitter **97**
Sandford 88
Sandford's Superb **88**
Sellers Cider **104**
Sellers, Norman 104
Sheppard, Gary 23
Sheppys Cider 67–68
Shepton Mallet 60
Sherston Scorcher **104**
Ship and Plough 21–22
SIBA 29, 54
Sidmouth 36
Silverton Inn 23
Simpson-Wells, Steve 76
Sleeper Heavy **19**
Smiles Best Bitter **82**
Smiles Brewery Bitter **82**
Smiles Brewing Company Limited 81–84
Somerset Dorset Railway Beer **53**
South Molton 38
Special **7**, **99**
St. Austell 9–10
St. Austell Brewery Company Ltd. 9–10
Station Porter **84**
Steam Brewery 7
stone flagons 63
Stone, Simon 6
stout 77, 78, 82, 98
Street 68
Summer Lightning **99**
Summerskills Best Bitter **29**
Summerskills Brewery 29–31
Sunbeam **52**
Swindon 92, 93

T

U

V

W

X

Y